Finding Comfort and Peace at a Difficult Time

HOPE BEYOND GRIEF

FINDING
COMFORT AND
PEACE AT A
DIFFICULT TIME

DEREK PRINCE

HOPE BEYOND GRIEF
Finding Comfort and Peace at a Difficult Time
By Derek Prince

This edition DPM-UK 2018

This book is taken from the transcripts of the following teaching series: "Victory Over Death" (015-017)

978-1-78263-623-6 Pub
978-1-78263-624-3 ePub
978-1-78263-625-0 Kindle
Bookcode B131

Derek Prince Ministries · www.derekprince.com
Set in Arno by Raphael Freeman, Renana Typesetting
Cover photo: Lina Trochez (Unsplash)

Contents

Foreword

Derek Prince taught people how to live triumphantly and effectively through the practical application of the Word of God. But Derek also taught people how to face the "last enemy" – death – in a hopeful way, always keeping a firm focus on the promise in Scripture of the ultimate victory of Jesus Christ.

Along with his extensive biblical understanding of how to face death victoriously, Derek had a wealth of experience from which he drew valuable insights. As a British soldier and hospital attendant, serving in northern Africa during World War II, he saw more than his share of the reality of death. Many years later, Derek went through the pain of losing his first wife, Lydia, in 1975, and then his second wife, Ruth, in 1998.

In addition, Derek had his own encounters with life-threatening illnesses during his lifetime.

As Derek has pointed out in this teaching, death is one of the toughest challenges we all must face at some point – one last foe, and an inevitable appointment none of us can avoid. However, he makes it clear that there can be great victory as we confront this ultimate enemy. The purpose of this message is to instill courage and inspiration in us, as we face the reality of death in our own experience. Our goal in providing this material is to bring you substantive comfort and hope – especially if you have just recently faced, or may now be facing, the loss of a loved one.

Derek Prince addresses a challenging but necessary topic for each of us. We trust that his clear teaching will give you a solid foundation on which to stand firmly and victoriously at the time when you need it most.

THE INTERNATIONAL PUBLISHING
TEAM OF DEREK PRINCE MINISTRIES

Chapter 1
The Universal Appointment

In this booklet, we will be dealing with a theme that is of vital importance for every one of us – without a single exception. Our theme is *Hope beyond grief.*

Let me ask you a question before we even begin our discussion. Is there something in you that flinches just for a moment at the mention of the word "death?" Is your first reaction a strong desire to lay this book aside? If so, that reaction is a sure indication that what is written here *is* for you. We trust you will benefit greatly from this message.

Present-Day Attitudes

In our contemporary culture, there has been a concerted effort to remove anything unpleasant or painful from the concept of death. For instance, there have been subtle changes in terminology. We no longer speak about a funeral home. Instead we use phrases like "a chapel of rest" or a funeral parlor. We no longer speak about a cemetery. Instead we call it "a memorial park." Then, when the body of a dead person is displayed for viewing before burial, cosmetic changes are made to minimize any physical effects caused by death.

I have heard psychological arguments offered in support of these efforts to soften the effects of death. Although I am not interested in contesting these arguments, I am concerned that we not forget one simple, objective, unchanging fact: **death is real.** It is our final foe – and our toughest challenge of all.

Nothing can change the fact that death is unpleasant, painful, and cruel. Any view of life that cannot accept this fact is deceptive and unrealistic. In addition, any philosophy or religion that does not have a positive answer to the reality of death is inadequate to meet the needs of humanity. One of the great distinguishing marks of the Christian faith, in contrast to other religions and philosophies, is that it has a positive, proven answer to death.

A Defeated Enemy

To approach this challenging subject of death, we will build our foundation upon Scriptural teaching and personal observation. The majority of what we present will be an examination of Scriptures dealing with death. The overall theme will be based upon what is found in 1 Corinthians 15:26, where Paul says, "The last enemy . . . is death." Death is an enemy – the universal enemy of the whole human race. However, through our examination of the Word of God, we will see that this enemy has been thoroughly defeated.

Another perspective by which I will address the subject of death is my own personal experience. Having lived a long time, I have, of course, experienced the loss of close relatives and loved ones: father, mother, and grandparents, to name a few. Most painful of all, I lost my two beloved wives – first Lydia, and then Ruth. With Lydia, I had shared many years of happy marriage. Equally happy and productive was my marriage to Ruth; so her passing was also a very hard experience for me. But God brought me through those times in victory by His grace. One of my hopes in presenting these truths and experiences is to help you face this reality in victory as well.

We can all rejoice in the fact that there is a resurrection to come. I believe in this resurrection! You see, I have two wives waiting for me on the other side! (I did not marry them both at the same time, but one after the other.) I was married to Lydia for thirty years and then Ruth for twenty years – so altogether, I was married for fifty years. The wonderful truth is that I am going to see them both again!

I will also be sharing from personal observation. During World War II, I served as a medical attendant on the battlefields and in the hospitals of North Africa. As you can imagine, I witnessed the death of many combatants during that service. Then later, as a minister, it was my frequent duty to counsel and help bereaved parishioners. So, in addressing this topic, I am not speaking merely from theory or from ministerial training, but from the realities of my life.

Returning to the faithful record of Scripture, we will explore what the Bible has to say about this theme. Hebrews 9:27 tells it like it is:

> *"And as it is appointed for men to die once, but after this the judgment."*

I have heard it said, *You may miss every appointment you ever made while you live, but there are two appointments you're going to keep: the first is death; the second is judgment.*

Someone once made this comment regarding the resurrection of Jesus: *Jesus is the only Person who made an appointment beyond the grave and kept it.* He is unique in that way (and many other ways too) because He was resurrected. All those who believe in Him will also be resurrected. We will be called forth from the grave.

We can thank God for Jesus, who is so faithful to tell us the truth! We can also thank God that Jesus is the remedy, as we will see in the next chapter.

Chapter 2
Our Redeemer

We cannot talk about the remedy for death without looking at the Bible's portrayal of Jesus. We will begin by looking at the purpose for which Jesus came:

> *"For this purpose the Son of God was manifested, that He might destroy the works of the devil".*
> (1 John 3:8)

What were the works of the devil? Scripture is clear in John 10:10 that the devil comes to steal, to kill, and to destroy. The Son of God, on the other hand, came to undo everything the devil has done against us. We need a clear vision of this truth: Jesus is the life-giver; and Satan is the life-taker.

Son of Man

In order to fulfill the purpose for which He came, Jesus had to identify Himself with us as a member of the human race. One of the favorite titles He used more than any other in reference to Himself in the gospels is "Son of Man," or "Son of Adam." Jesus was making a clear identification of Himself as a descendant of Adam – part of the human race. This is plainly stated in Hebrews 2:14, NIV:

> *"Since the children have flesh and blood, He too* [Jesus] *shared in their humanity so that by His death He might break the power of him who holds the power of death – that is, the devil..."*

Please notice the clear delineation of the two persons and responsibilities cited earlier. Satan is the one who wields the power of death. Jesus came to defeat him, to destroy him, and to break his power: **"and free those who all their lives were held in slavery by their fear of death"** (Hebrews 2:15, NIV).

As long as people are afraid of dying, they are in slavery. Why? Because the threat of death can compel them to do things they would never otherwise do. The fear of death is the ultimate form of slavery. Jesus came to set us free from that slavery, which is the fear of death. Since we, in our human nature, are made of flesh and blood, He shared our humanity:

> *"For this reason he had to be made like them, fully human in every way,"*
>
> (Hebrews 2:17a, NIV)

It is clear that Jesus became like us in every way, without ceasing to be divine. He became a member of the human race, the Son of Man. In this way, He was qualified to be what the Bible calls our "kinsman-redeemer." This is a very important concept introduced in the Old Testament, which is carried forward in the New Testament. It is one of the most vivid and beautiful prophetic pictures of Jesus found in the Old Testament.

The Kinsman-Redeemer

Let me give you a brief explanation of the "kinsman-redeemer." The Hebrew word for this role is *ga'al,* which is translated in a variety of ways depending on its context. Various translations are: *avenger* or *revenger of blood, redeemer, next kinsman* or *near kinsman*. As "redeemer," the Hebrew word *ga'al* is applied to God almost twenty times in the Old Testament.

Under the Law of Moses and the culture of Israel during Old Testament times, the kinsman-redeemer had two main responsibilities. If a man had been murdered, the first responsibility of the kinsman-redeemer was to see that the murderer was put to death. This obligation is stated in Numbers 35:19: "The avenger of blood [the *ga'al*] himself shall put the murderer to death." Second, if the man who had been murdered was married, and had died without offspring, the kinsman-redeemer was expected to take his widow as his own wife and raise up descendants for the dead man.

This second responsibility of the *ga'al* or the kinsman-redeemer is beautifully illustrated in the story of Ruth. Ruth the Moabitess, followed her mother-in-law, Naomi, when she went back to Bethlehem. Naomi told Ruth that she had a near kinsman in that region whose name was Boaz, a wealthy and influential man. Ruth went to glean in the fields of Boaz, and a relationship was established between them which led to marriage.

But before Boaz could marry Ruth, it was required that the property of the dead man be bought back for future descendants. Then he could marry the widow and raise up descendants on behalf of the victim – all of this was to ensure that the dead man's name would not be blotted out in Israel.

So, those are the two responsibilities of the *ga'al*, the kinsman-redeemer. First, to avenge the murder of his kinsman and second, to buy back his kinsman's inheritance, marry his kinsman's widow, and raise up descendants to carry on the family name.

Jesus: Our Redeemer

Earlier we stated that Jesus came as our *ga'al*, or our kinsman-redeemer. How did He fulfill His responsibilities in that capacity? First of all, He went against the murderer, Satan, and put an end to his power over us. He was the avenger against the one who was responsible for our death. Second, He took the Church to Himself as His bride, just as Boaz married Ruth, and thus restored to us our lost inheritance.

In John 10:10, we saw that Satan was the thief who came to steal. But Jesus said, "I have come that they may have life, and that they may have it more abundantly." In this way, Jesus overcame death and gave us back our inheritance. Now we have a new inheritance, an eternal inheritance in Jesus Christ.

Condemnation is gone. Fear of death is gone. We can say with the apostle John,

> *"The darkness is passing away, and the true light is already shining".* (1 John 2:8)

Our kinsman-redeemer has come and taken us to Himself. Jesus has avenged our "death" at Satan's hands, and restored to us our rightful inheritance in God's family.

Please take a few moments to meditate upon this statement, proclaiming it aloud until it becomes real to you: "Jesus has freed me from the fear of death and restored me to my eternal inheritance."

Chapter 3
The Resurrection

The greatest testimony to the power of Jesus Christ over death is His resurrection. It is the greatest event of all history up to this time – it is the very heart of Christianity. In truth, without the resurrection there is no Christian message. Everything revolves around the death, and the resurrection of Jesus Christ.

What Jesus accomplished is not a philosophy or a theory, but a fact of history. Theories and philosophies have little power to help humanity. But thank God, the resurrection is an eternal, historical truth.

> *"Moreover, brethren, I declare to you the gospel which I preached to you, which also you*

received and in which you stand, by which also you are saved, if you hold fast that word which I preached to you – unless you believed in vain. For I delivered to you first of all that which I also received: that Christ died for our sins according to the Scriptures, and that He was buried, and that He rose again the third day according to the Scriptures," (1 Corinthians 15:1–4)

Three Central Facts

What are the three central facts concerning Jesus Christ which make up the Gospel? First, He *died*. Second, He was *buried*. And third, He *rose again* on the third day. These truths need to be imprinted upon your mind and heart in such a way that you will never forget them.

Paul said, in writing to the Corinthian Christians: "These are the facts by which you are saved – unless you believed in vain". The warning he was conveying to them was that if they should depart from these basic facts in favor of religious theories, fantasies, or subjective experiences, then they would have believed in vain. I encourage you to take this opportunity, by the power of the

Holy Spirit, to indelibly imprint on your heart and mind these three key central statements that make up the Gospel: Christ died, He was buried, and He rose again on the third day.

These truths became reality to me in 1941 while I was serving as a soldier in the British army. I had a direct, personal revelation of Jesus one night in my barrack room. At that time, I was not unduly religious. Nor was I seeking something special, fanciful, or out of order. There was nothing unusual in my psychology at that moment. But Jesus revealed Himself to me so genuinely and so personally that, from that day to this, I have never doubted that He is alive. For me, knowing that He is alive is the most important fact of all.

How Christianity is Different

In connection with what Paul says about the three facts of the Gospel, let me point out three ways Christianity differs from almost every other major religion. The first is that Christianity is totally focused on a person: Jesus of Nazareth. The entire Gospel is centered on His life, death, and resurrection.

A second distinctive fact about Christianity is that it is rooted in history. As already emphasized, it is not floating in some misty realm of subjective truth, theory, or theology. It is grounded directly in human history.

The third fact of Christianity is that it is verified in the personal experience of those who believe – those who base their lives around these three vital truths: Christ's death, His burial, and His resurrection. Believing in these facts about Jesus produces a tremendous, supernatural transformation in the lives of anyone who takes this step of faith.

What should our response be? For the answer to that question, let's look at a beautiful passage describing the response of the women who were the first witnesses of the resurrection:

> *So they went out quickly from the tomb with fear and great joy, and ran to bring His disciples word. And as they went to tell His disciples, behold, Jesus met them, saying, "Rejoice!" So they came and held Him by the feet and worshiped Him.*
>
> (Matthew 28:8–9)

What else can we do when we realize who Jesus is, and what He did? There is no other reasonable response but to do as those women did – fall at His feet and worship Him. We take this attitude of worship with us into our next chapter as we discover what the Lord's resurrection means for each of us.

Chapter 4
Three Vital Truths

In Chapter 2, I explained how Jesus, as our kinsman-redeemer, took upon Himself the sentence of death that was due to us. He yielded up His soul as the sin offering on our behalf, thereby atoning for our guilt. Then on the third day, God the Father set aside the unjust decisions of the two human courts (Jewish and Roman) that had condemned Jesus to death. God vindicated the righteousness of his Son by raising Him from the dead.

In this chapter, we want to explore three vital truths from Jesus' resurrection – and their significance to all believers.

What the Resurrection Means

The first truth we need to see is that the resurrection of Jesus, who was our representative, is *the* sure seal upon God's offer of forgiveness and salvation.

The second truth is that Christ's resurrection is the guarantee of our resurrection:

> *"And He* [Jesus] *is the head of the body, the church, who is the beginning, the firstborn from the dead, that in all things He may have the preeminence".* (Colossians 1:18)

The resurrection of Jesus is our guarantee that we who are united with Him by faith will also be resurrected as He was. We will share in His resurrection.

The third truth about the resurrection is that it is the goal of our Christian living. The resurrection is a goal that we have to aim at continually. Paul is our example for pursuing that goal:

> *Not that I have already attained, or am already perfected; but I press on, that I may lay hold of that for which Christ Jesus has also laid hold of me.* (Philippians 3:12)

Our Attitude

What was Paul's attitude toward the resurrection of the dead? He was a mature apostle with a record of tremendous successes. Even so, he did not assume he had already attained that resurrection. Instead, he made it his purpose in life.

In effect, Paul is saying, nothing is going to stand between me and the fulfillment of Christ's purpose for me. I am going to press toward that mark. I am going to press onward and upward, and nothing is going to hold me back or deflect me from my supreme ambition, which is to attain to the resurrection from the dead.

How can our attitude be any different? How can we assume something Paul would not assume? We should each cultivate this same attitude as Paul – to press toward the goal, make it our purpose to attain it, and let nothing stand between us and the fulfillment of our purpose. I believe this is the challenge of the resurrection for each of us.

In our next chapter, we will look at the victory every believer receives from the resurrection of Jesus.

Chapter 5
Victory Over All Enemies

Christ's resurrection assures us of our victory over all our enemies – particularly over death. Any religion that does not have a satisfactory answer to death cannot meet humanity's deepest needs. Personally, I believe Christianity is the only religion which has this answer. And it comes by way of the death and resurrection of Jesus Christ.

The Resurrected Victor

A glorious picture of Christ as the resurrected victor is found in the book of Revelation. This is how Jesus appeared to the apostle John on the Isle of Patmos:

I was in the Spirit on the LORD*'s Day, and I heard behind me a loud voice as of a trumpet, saying, "I am the Alpha and the Omega, the First and the Last." ... Then I turned to see the voice that spoke with me. And having turned I saw seven golden lampstands, and in the midst of the seven lampstands One like the Son of Man. His countenance was like the sun shining in its strength. And when I saw Him, I fell at His feet as dead. But He laid His right hand on me, saying to me, "Do not be afraid; I am the First and the Last. I am He who lives, and was dead, and behold, I am alive forevermore. Amen. And I have the keys of Hades and of Death".*
(Revelation 1:10–11a, 12–13a, 16b–18)

This passage is a description of the resurrected Christ: "His feet were like fine brass... His voice as the sound of many waters ... His head and His hair were white like wool ... His eyes like a flame of fire ... out of His mouth went a sharp two-edged sword."

It is significant for us to remember that before the resurrection of Jesus, John the Apostle actually rested his head on Jesus' chest. He had been that close and relaxed with Him. But when John encountered the resurrected, glorified Christ, he was totally overcome. John himself says, "I became like one dead." That reveals the measure of the power and the glory displayed in the resurrected Christ.

Death Defeated

We know from our study that through the resurrection of Jesus, death has been defeated. Jesus has taken the sting from death.

> *For this corruptible must put on incorruption, and this mortal must put on immortality. So when this corruptible has put on incorruption, and this mortal has put on immortality, then shall be brought to pass the saying that is written: "Death is swallowed up in victory"* [Christ's victory has swallowed up death.]. *"O Death, where is your sting? O Hades, where is your victory?" The sting of death is sin, and the strength of sin is the law. But thanks be to God, who gives us the victory through our Lord Jesus Christ.*
>
> (1 Corinthians 15:53–57)

Jesus has taken away the sting from death. Death is now a servant of God's purposes – a defeated enemy waiting to be destroyed.

From Death to Life

In light of Christ's victory over death, I want to point out some promises Jesus gave in anticipation of His victory. When He uses the phrase "most assuredly," it introduces a statement that is absolutely authoritative.

> *Most assuredly, I say to you, he who hears My word and believes in Him who sent Me has everlasting life, and shall not come into judgment, but has passed from death into life.* (John 5:24)

Please notice that this truth is stated as something which has already taken place. It is not something that is going to happen in the future. By our belief and faith in the death and resurrection of Jesus Christ, we have already passed from death into life. Death has no more dominion over us, and no more claims against us. Death is merely the gateway into a new life. In John 8:51–52, we have this promise from Jesus Himself: "Most assuredly, I say to you, if anyone keeps My word he shall never see death. . . . If anyone keeps My word he shall never taste death."

Can you believe this truth for yourself and your loved ones? It is a promise from the lips of Jesus. He does not say that we will never experience physical death. But He says that those two evil angels, Death and Hades, have no more claim upon us. Their former dominion over us is excluded by the name and the blood of Jesus. When we face death, we are not going *down* into a kingdom of darkness. Rather, we are going *up* into the very presence of God. This is guaranteed for us by our belief in Jesus Christ.

Chapter 6
The Resurrection of Believers

The second coming of Jesus Christ is another New Testament topic that affirms the resurrection of righteous believers.

There are as many different prophecies in the Bible relating to the return of Christ as there are interpretations of what is going to take place. Rather than go into the controversial aspects of this subject, I would like to list five main purposes that the coming (or the return) of Jesus will fulfill. I am not suggesting that they are the only purposes, nor that they will necessarily take place in this order:

1. Jesus will receive the Church as His bride.
2. Israel as a nation will be saved.
3. Satan and the Antichrist will be overthrown.
4. The gentile nations will be judged.
5. Christ's millennial kingdom on earth will be established.

Resurrection of the Righteous Dead

As an integral part of the return of Jesus, the resurrection of righteous believers will take place. Speaking by revelation, this is how Paul describes it:

> *But I do not want you to be ignorant, brethren, concerning those who have fallen asleep, lest you sorrow as others who have no hope. For if we believe that Jesus died and rose again, even so God will bring with Him those who sleep in Jesus* [that is, those who have died in the faith]. *For this we say to you by the word of the Lord, that we who are alive and remain until the coming of the Lord will by no means precede those who are asleep. For the Lord Himself will descend from heaven with a shout, with the*

voice of an archangel, and with the trumpet of God. And the dead in Christ will rise first. Then we who are alive and remain shall be caught up together with them in the clouds to meet the Lord in the air. And thus we shall always be with the Lord. Therefore comfort one another with these words. (1 Thessalonians 4:13–18)

We need to bear in mind that these are words of comfort for us, and we can receive them as such.

We Shall Be Changed

This same event is described again by Paul in 1 Corinthians:

Behold, I tell you a mystery: We shall not all sleep, but we shall all be changed – in a moment, in the twinkling of an eye, at the last trumpet. For the trumpet will sound, and the dead will be raised incorruptible, and we [who are still alive on earth at the time] *shall be changed.* (1 Corinthians 15:51–52)

The word *sleep* is only used in these Scriptures of those who die in the faith, because it speaks of an awakening. What a dramatic event that will be!

I love that phrase, "in the twinkling of an eye." It means that at one moment you and I, as believers, will be looking at one another – then there will be a flash of brilliant light that will cause us to blink for just a moment. When we open our eyes again, we will see one another as completely different. In that split second, our physical bodies will have been totally transformed by the supernatural power of God. That is the glorious hope that lies ahead for every true believer.

We Shall Be Like Him

> *Beloved, now we are children of God; and it has not yet been revealed what we shall be, but we know that when He is revealed, we shall be like Him, for we shall see Him as He is.*
>
> (1 John 3:2)

Already we are the children of God by the inward life we have:

> *Christ in you, the hope of glory.*
>
> (Colossians 1:27)

But the full manifestation of that life in our external person will only happen when Jesus comes in His glory. Then we will be like Him. We will receive a body like His, because we shall see Him as He is.

There will be a revelation of the resurrected, glorified Christ to the believers who are waiting for Him that will be transforming in its power. That revelation will transform our mortal bodies into immortal bodies, our weak bodies into strong bodies, our bodies of humiliation into bodies of glory, our corruptible bodies into incorruptible bodies.

Paul says it like this in Philippians 3:21:

> *...according to the working by which He* [Jesus] *is able even to subdue all things to Himself.*

Do you believe that? Do you believe Jesus can subdue all things to Himself – even these weak, corruptible, frail bodies of ours? The Lord says we will be like Him – that our bodies will be brought into the likeness of His glorious body.

If we take these wonderful words to heart, they will continually encourage us and inspire us in this matter of facing death victoriously.

Chapter 7
How to Face Death

We have seen from previous chapters that our destiny will depend on one factor: our personal relationship with Jesus Christ. Jesus is the watershed and determining factor for all human existence. Faith in Jesus assures us of pardon, peace, and eternal life. On the other hand, rejection of Jesus in unbelief will ensure eternal judgment and condemnation by God.

In this chapter, we will make a very personal and practical application of these truths. Before we start, let me remind you once more that one of the appointments you are not going to miss is the one I am addressing now. I make the assertion in this chapter that if you are to face death with peace, confidence, and calm assurance, there are four main steps you must take.

Face It!

First, you have to face it. Face the fact that *you* are going to die, *I* am going to die, *each one* of us is going to die. As a minister, I am often amazed at how few people are prepared for death. People go through life knowing full well that they are going to die, yet never make adequate preparation for that inevitable event. It is not morbid to face the fact that you and I are going to die. It is simply being realistic. On the other hand, it is very unrealistic to live out your life without making preparation for what will unavoidably come at the end.

Consider what Paul says about himself in Philippians 1:21: "For to me, to live is Christ, and to die is gain."

Paul was not afraid of dying. He had faced the realities of sin, of judgment, and of God's requirements for his life. Because he had been willing to face them, he had passed into a relationship with God where there was no more fear. There was only a keen desire to be released from the bondage of this fleshly life and to enter into the fullness of God's presence.

Every one of us can have this same calm assurance that Paul carried. We can say as Paul said, "To live is Christ, but to die is gain."

Accept God's Offer

Facing death leads to the second step: accept God's offer of pardon, peace, and eternal life. Then you can say with Paul:

> *Therefore, having been justified by faith, we have peace with God through our Lord Jesus Christ.*
> (Romans 5:1)

For us to be justified, we must put our faith in the sacrificial death of Jesus Christ, acknowledging that He bore the guilt of our sin. What is it to be justified? Justified is "just-as-if-I'd never sinned." I have a righteousness imputed to me that has never known sin – the righteousness of Jesus Christ. In that righteousness I can face God, death, and eternity without a tremor or a fear.

Please notice what is said in 1 John 5:13:

These things I have written to you who believe in the name of the Son of God, that you may know that you have eternal life.

It is not merely that we believe, but that through believing we can come to know.

You may think, "I believe in Jesus." But I want to ask you, "Do you *know*?" The end purpose of believing is *knowing*. When we believe the way God requires us to believe in Jesus Christ, we also *know* that we have eternal life. We have it now. When death comes, it cannot touch or destroy the eternal life we already have in Jesus Christ.

Dedicate Yourself to Christ's Service

The third step is to dedicate yourself to Christ's service in this world. "For we must all appear before the judgment seat of Christ, that each one may receive the things done while in the body, whether good or bad" (2 Corinthians 5:10, NIV). There are only two categories for what we do in this life: good or bad. Anything that is not positively good is positively bad. We have to dedicate ourselves to Christ in such a way that what we do is good and acceptable to God.

How do we determine if what we are doing is good? The following questions will help. Are we pursuing our own self-satisfaction, or are we sincerely motivated by the desire for God's glory? Are we serving God on His terms or on ours? Are we serving God in our own power or in His power?

Wean Yourself from the Constraints of This World

The fourth step takes a little more explaining, but it is very important. It is to let God wean you from the constraints of the world around us. We must set our hearts on the excellence that is beyond this world and in the next. This is how God weans us from the constraints of this present time.

The Bible is very realistic. It says: "If only for this life we have hope in Christ, we are of all people most to be pitied" (1 Corinthians 15:19, NIV). Does faith in Christ extend beyond this world? If not, our religion is a pitiful imagination. If our hope in Christ is genuine, it does not cease with this life. It gets brighter and brighter throughout eternity.

This hope produces a lifestyle that is different. Paul admonishes us in Colossians 3:1 to set our hearts and our minds "on things above." The ultimate reward for all believers is beyond the constraints of this world. Our true life, which is Christ, will be manifested in its glory and fullness beyond the grave.

The Appointed Time

Death does not need to be an accident that comes untimely or too soon. If we are moving in the purposes of God, we can prepare ourselves and approach death like a sheaf that is ripe in its season, to be gathered by the Lord in its appointed time. This is the promise of Job 5:26: "You will come to the grave in full vigor, like sheaves gathered in season" (NIV).

At the end of World War II, Lydia and I were living north of Jerusalem in Ramallah – which was then a quiet, Christian Arab town. In that town there was an Arab woman, a believer, who died. When Lydia saw the woman's grandson, she asked, "What did she die of?" The grandson thought for a moment, and then he answered, "She didn't die of anything. She was ripe, that's all."

What a beautiful answer! How are you going to die? Ripe or unripe? Remember you do not have to die sick. There are very few believers in the Bible of whom it is recorded that they died sick. If you live the Bible way, you die – not because you are sick, but because you are ripe.

Not only can we face our own death in this manner, but we can believe the same for a loved one. We can be comforted and at peace, even as we face the death of the ones who are dear to us.

Chapter 8

Facing the Death of a Loved One

I believe there are some truths a person can only understand by experiencing them. This became true for me in 1975 when the Lord called home my first wife, Lydia. We had been happily married for thirty years. During that time, we had shared everything – poverty, riches, bad times, and good times. Together we had raised a family of nine adopted girls while also serving the Lord in ministry. Sometimes, after we had been ministering together in a service or a conference, people would come up to us and say, "You two work together just like one person."

That was the kind of unity there was between us. When the Lord called Lydia home, it was as if a part of me had also been taken away. For me, this was the most agonizing experience of my life.

I had a wonderful marriage with Lydia, but we were always in the midst of a large, busy family. However, God arranged my second marriage with Ruth differently. Most of our time together was just us by ourselves. For twenty years, we traveled, prayed, and worked by ourselves. I experienced an intimacy in my relationship with Ruth that I had never known with any other person – and never expect to experience again until I get to heaven.

Then, in December 1998, God called Ruth home as well. At the interment service for Ruth, as I was standing in front of the open grave looking down on her casket, I felt prompted to cry out, **"Father, I trust You! I thank You that You are always kind. You are always kind and loving and just. You never make a mistake. What You do is always the best."** That was one of the hardest proclamations I have ever made, and it was also one of the best.

Lessons Learned

After Ruth's passing, I began to observe that when bereaved men and women would approach me, I was able to comfort them in a way I had not been able to do before. As I comforted others, I realized that very few people are prepared for the death of a loved one. What I have discovered, however, is that we can face the death of a loved one in victory. It can be an experience where we see clear evidence of God's love and faithfulness to us.

On the basis of my experiences, I want to offer some counsel on what to do if and when you are faced with this situation.

1. ***Trust God's love and wisdom.*** There is a beautiful example of this trust in the story of Job. Job's seven sons and three daughters had all been taken by death in a moment – in a single disaster. But this is what Job said,

> *The LORD gave, and the LORD has taken away; blessed be the name of the LORD.* (Job 1:21)

I do not believe those words were said in resignation. I believe Job said this in trust.

If you can trust the Lord to give, can you not trust the Lord when He takes away? Can you not trust His wisdom? Doesn't God know the right way and right time to take each one of His children? I believe He does.

2. ***Yield your loved one to God.*** This is not an easy step. I remember how I felt about an hour after Lydia died. I said to the Lord, "I won't ask for her back. She was Yours before she was mine." When I said that, it was as if a barrier was pulled out of my heart. Saying those words made room for the hand of God to move in and begin healing the wound.

Likewise, when Ruth passed away, I said to God, "Father, I trust You." I decided to trust God and believe that He did what was best – both for Ruth and for me. I yielded to Him, and yielded Ruth to Him as well. My second word of counsel is: yield up your loved one.

3. ***Reaffirm your faith***. It may sound strange for a preacher to say this, but when God took my wives, each time I had to ask myself, "Do I really believe what I have been preaching all these

years? Do I really believe there will be a resurrection? Do I really believe I will see them again?"

For a while, it was hard for me to answer. Then one day, I was able to say, "I do believe. I have not put my faith in beliefs that are unreal and insubstantial. I have put my faith in truths which will stand every test – the faithfulness of God, the love of God, and the validity of Scripture."

When you are faced with this situation, reaffirm your faith. Every time you do so, your faith will be strengthened. You will walk in greater victory.

4. ***Express your emotions.*** Don't bottle up your feelings! Don't try to be stoical. Stoicism is a pagan philosophy that originated in Greece. The stoic was the one who would not let anything hurt him. He was so in control of himself that he never laughed or cried. In fact, he never showed his emotions.

Such an absence of response has nothing to do with the Christian faith. God knows we are human beings. Scripture says He knows what we are made of. He knows our feelings and our thoughts. God knows you are hurting. He knows you are experiencing grief. He is not angry with you for having these feelings.

I have always been impressed with the fact that in the history of Israel, after they lost their two great leaders – Moses and Aaron – God allowed them a period of mourning (see Deuteronomy 34:8–12 and Numbers 20:23–29) In each case, God permitted Israel thirty days to mourn them. He knew that the Israelites could not just get up and go on as though nothing had happened. The Lord knew they were going to miss these leaders who had been taken out of their lives. So He instructed them to take thirty days and express their feelings – don't bottle it up.

We have to be honest and realistic. We need to admit that we are grieving and it hurts. I have found that God heals our hurt when we expose it to Him with honesty. If you try to bottle up your feelings, they will just go inward where they will fester – possibly producing an emotional problem later on. From expressing my grief honestly and openly, I became a healthier and stronger person, both mentally and emotionally, than I was before I went through those experiences, both with Lydia and with Ruth.

5. ***Lean on your fellow believers.*** In 1 Thessalonians 4:18, Paul challenges us: "Therefore comfort one another with these words." There are times when we need comfort from our fellow believers. One blessing I will never forget is the love that was shown to me by countless friends, family, and church members.

In looking back, I thank God that I was part of a Christian body – a committed group of believers who shared their lives with each other. Believe me, when your hour of crisis comes, you need people to comfort you. We all face times when we need committed believers who will stand by us.

6. ***Continue to serve Christ as faithfully as you can.*** Do not let anything hold you back from your own personal obligation to the Lord – to serve Him and to fulfill the ministry He has given you.

> *Brethren, I do not count myself to have apprehended; but one thing I do, forgetting those*

things which are behind and reaching forward to those things which are ahead, I press toward the goal for the prize of the upward call of God in Christ Jesus. (Philippians 3:13–14)

One of the secrets of successful Christian living is to be able to forget what lies behind and reach forward to what lies ahead. There is a prize ahead! Press toward it!

A Wonderful Assurance

The prize before us is an eternity in the presence of Almighty God. That prize has been guaranteed to all who have placed their trust in Jesus Christ. When we believe in the death and resurrection of Jesus Christ, we have already passed from death into life. Death has no more dominion over us – no more claims against us. Death is merely the gateway into a new life.

This truth was probably best expressed by the well-known evangelist, Billy Graham, with the following quote:

"Someday you will read or hear that Billy Graham is dead. Don't you believe a word of it. I shall be more alive than I am now. I

will just have changed my address. I will have gone into the presence of God."

As I look back on my life and the times of mourning I faced, I see them as yet another proof of God's love and faithfulness. Now, as I find myself in my late eighties, I know that I will soon come to the end of my life's journey. I am not afraid at all. I look forward to all the glories in the life to come – and the many people I will meet (and see again!) in Heaven.

This theme of facing death victoriously is both real and practical to me. I trust that you now have the assurance that Christ will give you that same victory – that by His grace, you will find hope and comfort for the toughest challenge of all.

Perhaps the best way to end this book would be for us to pray a simple prayer together, asking the Lord to help us.

Dear Lord,

I confess that the topic of death is troubling and perplexing to me. But I desire to face it – for myself and my loved ones – with peace and confidence. I ask for that now.

I also ask for Your divine comfort in the sorrow I am facing over the loss of a loved one. I open my heart to You, Lord, to receive Your hope and victory.

In Jesus' name. Amen.

About the Author

Derek Prince (1915–2003) was born in India of British parents. He was educated as a scholar of Greek and Latin at Eton College and King's College, Cambridge in England. Upon graduation he held a fellowship (equivalent to a professorship) in Ancient and Modern Philosophy at King's College. Prince also studied Hebrew, Aramaic, and modern languages at Cambridge and the Hebrew University in Jerusalem. As a student, he was a philosopher and self-proclaimed agnostic.

Bible Teacher

While in the British Medical Corps during World War II, Prince began to study the Bible as a philosophical work. Converted through a powerful encounter with Jesus Christ, he was baptized in the Holy Spirit a few days later. Out of this encounter, he formed two conclusions: first, that Jesus Christ is alive; second, that the Bible is a true, relevant, up-to-date book. These conclusions altered the whole course of his life, which he then devoted to studying and teaching the Bible as the Word of God.

Discharged from the army in Jerusalem in 1945, he married Lydia Christensen, founder of a children's home there. Upon their marriage, he immediately became father to Lydia's eight adopted daughters – six Jewish, one Palestinian Arab, and one English. Together, the family saw the rebirth of the state of Israel in 1948. In the late 1950s, they adopted another daughter while Prince was serving as principal of a teacher training college in Kenya.

In 1963, the Princes immigrated to the United States and pastored a church in Seattle. In 1973, Prince became one of the founders of Intercessors for America. His book *Shaping History through Prayer and Fasting* has awakened Christians around the world to their responsibility to pray for their governments. Many consider underground translations of the book as instrumental in the fall of communist regimes in the USSR, East Germany, and Czechoslovakia.

Lydia Prince died in 1975, and Prince married Ruth Baker (a single mother to three adopted children) in 1978. He met his second wife, like his first wife, while she was serving the Lord in Jerusalem. Ruth died in December 1998 in Jerusalem, where they had lived since 1981.

Teaching, Preaching and Broadcasting

Until a few years before his own death in 2003 at the age of eighty-eight, Prince persisted in the ministry God had called him to as he traveled the world, imparting God's revealed truth, praying for the sick and afflicted, and sharing his prophetic insights into world events in the light of Scripture. Internationally recognized as a Bible scholar and spiritual patriarch, Derek Prince established a teaching ministry that spanned six continents and more than sixty years. He is the author of more than fifty books, six hundred audio teachings, and one hundred video teachings, many of which have been translated and published in more than one hundred languages.

He pioneered teaching on such groundbreaking themes as generational curses, the biblical significance of Israel, and demonology.

Prince's radio program, which began in 1979, has been translated into more than a dozen languages and continues to touch lives. Derek's main gift of explaining the Bible and its teaching in a clear and simple way has helped build a foundation of faith in millions of lives. His nondenominational, nonsectarian approach has made his teaching equally relevant and helpful to people from all racial and religious backgrounds, and his teaching is estimated to have reached more than half the globe.

DPM Worldwide Ministry

In 2002, he said, "It is my desire – and I believe the Lord's desire – that this ministry continue the work, which God began through me over sixty years ago, until Jesus returns."

Derek Prince Ministries International continues to reach out to believers in over 140 countries with Derek's teaching, fulfilling the mandate to keep on "until Jesus returns." This is accomplished through the outreaches of more than thirty Derek Prince offices around the world, including primary work in Australia, Canada, China, France, Germany, the Netherlands, New Zealand, Norway, Russia, South Africa, Switzerland, the United Kingdom, and the United States. For current information about these and other worldwide locations, visit www.derekprince.com.

ALSO RECOMMENDED FOR YOU

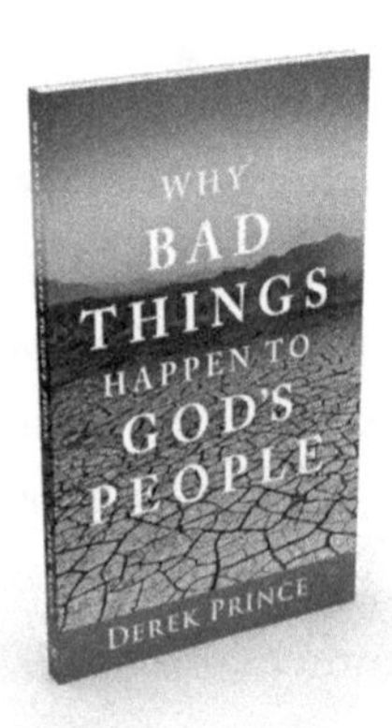

WHY BAD THINGS HAPPEN TO GOD'S PEOPLE

Have you ever asked:

"If God loves me, why am I going through this trial?" or

"Why is there so much misery, suffering, persecution and injustice in the world?"

God's people still experience the challenges of life. There is one factor, however, that sets people of faith apart – hope.

In this book, Derek Prince shares timeless truths from the book of Job that will keep you anchored during any storm.

£7.99
ISBN 978-1-782634-69-0
Paperback and e-book

www.dpmuk.org/shop

ALSO RECOMMENDED FOR YOU

THE THREE MOST POWERFUL WORDS: I FORGIVE YOU

Do you know the three most powerful words? According to Derek Prince, they are, 'I forgive you.'

The Bible clearly points out, that as long as you resist forgiving others, you allow the enemy legal access into your life. This can cause you damage and can even provoke God's anger. This book can help you to say, 'I forgive you', and mean it. It can enable you to see how God can empower your prayers, tear down hindrances to healing and open the pathway to receiving His blessings into your life.

£4.99
ISBN 978-1-78263-424-9
Paperback and e-book

www.dpmuk.org/shop

ALSO RECOMMENDED FOR YOU

ENTERING THE PRESENCE OF GOD

Using the Old Testament tabernacle as his illustration, supported by texts from Hebrews and other New Testament writings, Derek Prince shows the way to victorious intimacy with God and explains how you can enter into the very presence of God to receive the spiritual, physical, and emotional blessings of true worship.

£ 7.99
ISBN 978-1-901144-42-0
Paperback and eBook

www.dpmuk.org/shop

ALSO RECOMMENDED FOR YOU

SHARING IN CHRIST'S VICTORY OVER DEATH

The greatest event of all history up to this time is the resurrection of Jesus Christ. In fact, without the resurrection, there is no Christian message. If it is just a theory or a philosophy, it has no power to help humanity. But thank God, it is a fact of history!

In this book, Derek Prince shows the glorious victory of Jesus Christ over the powers of death and how his victory affects our lives today.

£7.99
ISBN 978-1-78263-494-2
Paperback and eBook

www.dpmuk.org/shop

MORE BEST-SELLERS BY DEREK PRINCE

Blessing or Curse: You Can Choose
Bought with Blood
Foundational Truths for Christian Living
Life-Changing Spiritual Power
Marriage Covenant
Prayers & Proclamations
Self-Study Bible Course
Shaping History Through Prayer and Fasting
Spiritual Warfare for the End Times
They Shall Expel Demons
Who Is the Holy Spirit?

Derek Prince Ministries Offices Worldwide

DPM – Asia/Pacific

38 Hawdon Street
Sydenham
Christchurch 8023
New Zealand
T: + 64 3 366 4443
E: admin@dpm.co.nz
W: www.dpm.co.nz and www.derekprince.in

DPM – Australia

15 Park Road
Seven Hills
New South Wales 2147
Australia
T: +61 2 9838 7778
E: enquiries@au.derekprince.com
W: www.derekprince.com.au

DPM – Canada
P.O. Box 8354 Halifax
Nova Scotia B3K 5M1
Canada
T: + 1 902 443 9577
E: enquiries.dpm@eastlink.ca
W: www.derekprince.org

DPM – France
B.P. 31, Route d'Oupia
34210 Olonzac
France
T: + 33 468 913872
E: info@derekprince.fr
W: www.derekprince.fr

DPM – Germany
Söldenhofstr. 10
83308 Trostberg
Germany
T: + 49 8621 64146
E: ibl@ibl-dpm.net
W: www.ibl-dpm.net

DPM – Netherlands
Nijverheidsweg 12
7005 BJ Doetinchem
Netherlands
T: +31 251–255044
E: info@derekprince.nl
W: www.derekprince.nl

DPM – Norway
P.O. Box 129
Lodderfjord
N-5881 Bergen
Norway
T: +47 928 39855
E: sverre@derekprince.no
W: www.derekprince.no

Derek Prince Publications Pte. Ltd.
P.O. Box 2046
Robinson Road Post Office
Singapore 904046
T: + 65 6392 1812
E: dpmchina@singnet.com.sg
W: www.dpmchina.org (English)
www.ygmweb.org (Chinese)

DPM – South Africa
P.O. Box 33367
Glenstantia
0010 Pretoria
South Africa
T: +27 12 348 9537
E: enquiries@derekprince.co.za
W: www.derekprince.co.za

DPM – Switzerland
Alpenblick 8
CH-8934 Knonau
Switzerland
T: + 41 44 768 25 06
E: dpm-ch@ibl-dpm.net
W: www.ibl-dpm.net

DPM – UK
PO Box 393
Hitchin SG5 9EU
United Kingdom
T: + 44 1462 492100
E: enquiries@dpmuk.org
W: www.dpmuk.org

DPM – USA

P.O. Box 19501
Charlotte NC 28219
USA
T: + 1 704 357 3556
E: ContactUs@derekprince.org
W: www.derekprince.org

CPSIA information can be obtained
at www.ICGtesting.com
Printed in the USA
BVHW040043170223
658667BV00007B/1084